# Making Money Through Live Events

## A Live Event Planning Workbook

Melissa Jakes

ISBN-10: 1981959122
ISBN-13: 978-1981959129

There are times I sit and wonder how I got into this situation. Fear, Doubt, and Worry seem to keep me there. Have you had a visit from FDW( Fear, Doubt, and Worry)? I have, and sometimes they come together but other times they come separate. How can these invisible things take my mind and make me doubt what I'm doing? When they come together I shut down.

But my daughter tells me, "Mom your awesome" or "My mommy is beautiful." After setting up for Thanksgiving dinner, she looks at me and says, "the leaves are so pretty mommy, great job!" That's it! That's when FDW starts to lift and starts to fly away; that's when I realized they're invisible and I remember they're invisible. FDW cannot stay in your mind, nor can they be involved in your business.

As an entrepreneur Fear, Doubt, and Worry are words that harm your business, will make your business fail, and kill, yes, kill your dreams. Hosting and/or planning an event can be seem overwhelming but it does not have to be.

This guide will help you organize yourself, keep yourself in budget, build your audience, and your brand. Each step will follow with reflection questions that I encourage you to answer. It will help you understand your vision, purpose and execution for your next epic event. Sometimes we need words of encouragement. Throughout this book, I provide words of affirmations to push away those FDW's and fill your heart, mind and soul with words of affirmations.

Be Purposeful

Be Strong

Be Creative

Be Mindful

And Remember Be You!

# CONTENTS

MELISSA JAKES

# ACKNOWLEDGMENTS

First, I would like to Thank God for all he has done! Secondly, to my husband and my daughter, thank you for allowing to prosper in my gift and providing me with all your support through this journey! To my parents, Thank you for always supporting me through my journey of life. To my brother, thank you supporting me and pushing me to go further than the norm. To my entrepreneur friends, Desiree Lee, Christina Dukes, Rashana Roach, LaNette Parson, and Shade Adu, Thank you for every opportunity and support along the way.

Let's Make An Epic Event!

# 1

# INTRODUCTION

I started off by planning weddings, baby showers, and sweet 16 parties, which I still love to do, but after successfully planning and executing my first conference, it opened my eyes. Planning a live event is more than just booking rooms for your keynotes speakers, table settings, and what type of food you will offer your guest.

Live events help influencers create income, exposure, publicity, increase their following, establish credibility, and move their businesses to the next level. As a busy influencer or entrepreneur, it is hard to keep up with the logistics of creating the timeline, organizing vendors and speakers, negotiations with venues and caterers, or most importantly missing out on the value due to lack of knowledge and industry experience.

*It's time to stop dreaming*

*about your Live Event*

*and start planning your Live Event.*

During my event planning years, I've learned that events can do more than just create jovial memories and celebrate a festive occasion. Event planning can also help entrepreneurs gain the exposure needed to grow their businesses.

Seeing the need for such event planning, I

created this guide for entrepreneurs, for profit-based organizations, and nonprofit organizations who are trying to grow their revenue, become more noticeable, develop a following, and create an event to showcase their brand.

This guide will help you organize yourself to properly prepare for a live event, learn how to market, bring people to your live event, and how to successfully execute your live event. I will personally guide you, throughout this book, on some of my best kept secrets and skills that I have gained along the way that will help you understand the behind the scenes of event planning and how to profit from creating an epic event.

2

# STEP: 1 SETTING THE FOUNDATION

You're trying to get your business out there, to woo some new clients, right? What better way for people to find out who you are and what exactly you have to offer, than simply telling them.

Putting on a live event is an excellent ways of getting your brand out there. Now is the time for you to branch out and create your first live event.

## NOW WHAT?!

Planning your first event can be scary, frightening, even intimidating; fortunately anything is possible with a plan. The amount of fear you'll encounter really depends on how big you want to jump.

Should you do a smaller event to start off, then grow your event to a bigger scale, or do you jump in and host your first annual conference that changes other people's lives forever?

Let's set a foundation for how we will plan our first event. Setting the foundation is very important and will guide you towards a prosperous event. I love using acronyms, as they make terms easier to remember, and this one will help you set your foundation for planning your event.

Contemplate these four areas before your next event!

**TBTW**:

T- Target Audience

B- Budgeting

T- Timeline

W- What if ?!


**Target Audience:**

Identify and understand your Target Audience. I cannot stress this enough. It is most important to understand who this event is for, and why your target audience should want to pay you to attend this event.


Ask yourself, what will they gain from this event, and how will it impact them. Understanding your purpose and the target audience will give you a better perspective of how you should lay the foundation for your event.

Tailor your event for your target audience. Remember that it's not about you, it's about your target audience and how they will benefit from it. I always remind my clients that if you want a venue that attracts attendees, you have to ask yourself, how will they get there? Is there free parking? Is the parking easily accessible? Is the venue conveniently near a bus or train station?

Attracting your target audience will take some research and polling on your part. Also, a simple test of trial and error will help you understand how they responds to you.

Do they like your content that you post on social media? Do they tune in every time you start a live recording on social media? Finding the answers to these questions will get you to understand how you should reach out to your target audience.

## Budgeting:

When planning your next epic event, setting a budget is mandatory! Going into an event NOT having a planned course of action, or NOT thinking about how you want your it to be, would be the most catastrophic mistake.

With that being said, you must set a realistic budget for the event. Having a range included into your budget is a great idea and setting the range within $1,000-$2,000 of your proposed budget is realistic when planning your event.

Utilizing Free Resources: The internet is such a magical resource. Most of us forget to use resources that are free or almost free. Did you know you could pay only $5.00-

$10.00 per month for quality graphic designing and marketing on social media.

Reaching out to universities or high schools that offer internship credits is a great way to gain free labor, and it provides valuable experience to the student worker. Collaborating with venues, photographers, videographers, and industry professionals is a great way to gain sponsorships for products that will help make your event a success.

Remember, the goal is to stay on budget, so taking the initiative to locate resources is the best way to stay on target.

**Timeline:**

Most people think of a timeline as an agenda; however a timeline is more than just what will happen during the event, it is also an accountability tool that can help streamline your future live events.

You should have two timelines; one timeline for your production (which includes how all the items will get completed to make your event successful) and a timeline for the day of the event. Be sure to include in your timeline the tasks that are delegated to your team with a date of completion, in order to hold people accountable, and to ensure the tasks get completed within the time frame allotted.

Having a pre-planning meeting, either virtually or in person, will get your team engaged, and they will be invested in the event. Give yourself at least a month before you schedule the event. This will ensure your audience has enough time to attend the event, and it will allow you the necessary time to create your epic money-making event.

## What Ifs ?!:

I love to have multiple backup plans, just in case life happens, which it will! Having a plan A, B, and C will ensure that you are thinking through your event. It will ensure that if something does arise, you have completely thought about how you can problem solve the issue.

Also, be sure to read through your contracts and agreements to be knowledgeable of the details of services that your speakers, vendors, and venues provide. For instance, if you have a catered event, having more people than your contract states may require you to inform the caterer so that they may make the appropriate accommodations.

Knowing what their backup/rainy day plan is will assist you in preparation for the "what-ifs". Some vendors or speakers have different types of clauses in their contracts/agreements and it is better to be safe than sorry.

Reflection Questions:

1. Write out your ideal TBTW.

_____

_____

_____

_____

_____

_____

_____

_____

_____

_____

2. How will you attract your target audience?

_____

_____

_____

_____

_____

_____

_____

_____

_____

_____

3. List some partnerships that you can collaborate with by planning this event.

_____

_____

_____

_____

_____

_____

_____

_____

_____

3

# STEP 2: GEARING UP

Now that you have set the foundation, you have a venue, a date, a budget, and an understanding of how you are going to prepare for the event production, it is now time to get into the minutia of the planning process.

This process will include booking speakers who will bring great content to your event, picking sponsors to offset your event costs, and bringing all aspects together, such as theme, branding colors, lighting, music, additional audiovisual equipment, etc.

It is important to check in with your speakers and special guests, regarding their presentations, to ensure all of their audiovisual and logistical needs will be accommodated. Ordering supplies in advance keeps yourself organized, prevents you from running around at the last moment, and allows time for special order items to be shipped on time.

As we all know specialized items take time to order, and it is advisable to consider what items may not be readily available so that we can get those products ordered as soon as possible.

Also, ordering extras supplies is always better than not having enough; this is especially useful for when it comes to the items like pens, folders, or welcome packets.

When you don't have enough items, it appears to the attendees that host was not organized or prepared for the event, and can give them the impression that you conduct all your business carelessly.

Reflection Questions:

1. What type of venue will be ideal for you?

   _____

   _____

   _____

   _____

   _____

   _____

   _____

   _____

   _____

2. When thinking of speakers, write out what type of speakers you would like,

and how you will do your speaker call?

_____

_____

_____

_____

_____

_____

_____

_____

3. How do you envision your venue space?

_____

_____

_____

_____

_____

_____

_____

_____

# 4

## STEP 3: MARKETING

Develop promotional materials! Develop promotional materials! Develop promotional materials! Marketing is one of the most important steps to a successful event. Using multiple marketing mediums will assist you in reaching your target audience, and it is the only way people will know who you are and what you are doing.

The goal is to get the public interested and eventually convert them into paying customers, this is how your will receive your

ROI (Return On Investment). There are different online applications that can help you create flyers, social media campaigns, and online webinars to help build the excitement about your event and getting the audience to learn more about you.

Develop a schedule for the campaign. Creating a schedule for how you will promote your event is very important, as the schedule will help you build the excitement without overwhelming your potential clients with too much content multiple times a day. Crowding your marketing on the schedule can create a sense of annoyance with your target audience, and can result in them not attending the event.

Release promotional pieces, press releases, and related materials in accordance with the schedule, with news releases preceding promotional mailings. Most people do not know that you can have a press release for any type of event. It gives the media world a better understanding on how to help you promote your event with all the proper information needed. Also spread the news of your event on the radio, via podcast, or television interviews; this will help you reach your target audience in ways you may not have thought of before. Reposting an interview that plugs your business on social media is also highly recommended.

Reflection Questions:

1. What does your marketing timeline look like?

   _____

   _____

   _____

   _____

   _____

   _____

   _____

   _____

2. Thinking of ROI, what do you want your ideal ROI to be?

_____

_____

_____

_____

_____

_____

_____

3. What does your marketing strategy plan look like? How will you accomplish it?

_____

_____

_____

_____

_____

_____

_____

5

## STEP 4: PREPARATION

Ordering items for your event will make up a bulk of this step. All of the items that will be needed for the event will need to be ordered a month in advance. If you're ordering signs and printed materials to be handouts or pass outs at the event, this should be ordered a month in advance.

Emailing attendees the basic overview of the event to get them excited, should be done at least one week out from the event. Also, mention the type of attire you would like the guest to wear, especially if the event is very formal (you wouldn't want your guests to be out of place).

In addition, inform vendors, speakers, volunteers, and staff members what to wear the day of and be sure to select the type of name badges you would like them to wear.

Confirm all audiovisual requirements. Ask all of your presenters to complete the request form for their audiovisual needs. Will they need a handheld microphone or a lapel microphone? Do they want music queued up for their walking on and off stage?

All these questions should be included in an a easy form (preferably on an online system that will allow them to fill it out) and the event planner/coordinator can review it as the forms are being completed.

Read over your timeline. Reviewing the timeline for the production over and over again will prevent many issues later in the planning process. Also, during this step, you should be finalizing the timeline for the day so that speakers, vendors, and the venue can start working on their items needed to ensure they arrive on time and prevent issues.

Reflection Questions:

1. Start thinking about how many volunteers you will need for this event. How will you place a call to action to attract the right volunteers for this event?

_____

_____

_____

_____

_____

_____

_____

_____

_____

2.  When will you have a meeting with
    the volunteers, and what items will be
    on your agenda?

_____

_____

_____

_____

_____

_____

_____

_____

_____

3. Write out the Run of the Show, and
   see what items are still missing.

   _____

_____

_____

_____

_____

_____

_____

_____

_____

_____

_____

MELISSA JAKES

# 6

# STEP: 5 BEFORE YOU GO LIVE

Review all details of your event. At least two weeks before your event, review and schedule a walkthrough of the venue with the event manager and/or event planner to ensure all aspect of the your event is fully ready to go.

Most venues have a banquet checklist to go over everything you ordered in your contract. It is important to review this checklist and make sure you visually confirm that everything is present. Don't be afraid to ask questions and advocate for yourself when dealing with vendors and venues, but please do so in the most professional way you can; after all you need them to help your event run smoothly.

Send the full agenda to all vendors, speakers, and anyone who will be assisting in the execution of this event. Keeping everyone on your team informed of the schedule will produce a smoother event and your attendees will notice the fluidity.

This ensures that everyone knows what time to arrive, to check in, and report to the event planner/coordinator. Make sure your schedule includes date, time, location, and who is conducting what.

Final check in. Check in with all vendors, speakers, volunteers, and staff the day before the event to ensure they will arrive on time and receive the event planner's/coordinators contact information for any questions or issues that might arise before the event.


Reflection Question:

1. What last minute items would you might need to pack? Remember to always pack an emergency kit (pens, tape, safety pins, bobby pins, needle and thread, etc.)

_____

_____

_____

_____

_____

_____

_____

_____

_____

7

# STEP 6: LIGHTS, CAMERA, ACTION!

You made it! It's event day! Inspect the venue space at least two hour in advance to ensure everything is in place and ready to go. Also, check the temperature of the meeting space to ensure it's not too hot or cold. When the temperature is not controlled, your attendees could start losing their focus if the room temperature is too hot or when it's too cold.

Make sure your event planner/coordinator is keeping you updated on major issues or changes, and keeping you and the event on time. Starting on time is a major part of the event! When people know that you started your events on time they will respect your brand and your business.

Make final payments. For all of the vendors and the venue, ensure that payments are paid up on event day. This builds credibility and rapport with your vendors, speaker, staff members, etc. Follow all contract due dates and, if problems occur with payments, have a real conversation with your vendor about creating a realistic timeline to make the final payments. Some companies are willing to agree to do a NET 15 or NET 30. This means they will accept payment 15 days after the event or 30 days after the event.

### *Smile You Made It!*

Enjoy your event and take it all in; watch how amazingly your event has been executed. Your brand and your business is on display for people to see how awesome you are and get to know you a little bit more!

Reflection Questions:

1. How do you feel after the event?

   _____

   _____

   _____

   _____

   _____

   _____

   _____

   _____

2. What did not go so well?

   _____

   _____

   _____

   _____

_____

_____

_____

_____

_____

_____

3.   What went very well?

_____

_____

_____

_____

_____

_____

_____

_____

_____

8

## STEP 7: THE FOLLOW UP, A SUCCESSFUL LIVE EVENT

Conduct a survey after your event. Survey's give you great anonymous feedback on the event, and give you input on how you can grow and get better as a brand. Your follow up surveys should only ask closed ended questions, but not necessarily just yes and no.

It should also include a comment section; mostly those that really loved or really hated your event will use this section (I'm sure you will receive mostly love). Surveys should be available virtually and should not be longer than one page.

Make time after your event to meet with the event planner/coordinator to review your event, including any charges that happened during the event, and go over all receipts for products sold during the event. Also, review lessons learned and debrief on what was beneficial and what was least beneficial.

Share with the event manager/planner the names of staff or vendor who have provided extraordinary service. Be sure that you share that information with staff members or vendors and shout them out for their hard work!

### *Promote Your Next Event!*

Promoting the success of your initial event

and showcasing how great the event went can help you in promoting future events. This is a great opportunity to inform the public of how they can get tickets to the next event.

Get testimonials from those who attended and share them during your marketing for your next event. People love to see other people's reactions and feedback on whether they should buy a product, and this theory works for events as well, especially when you conduct annual events.

If you're prepared to do so, promote and offer presale tickets or products at a discounted rate off your next year event for those who did attend. This will bring in higher ticket sales for your next event and create a buzz around it. Make sure this offer is limited, and the timeline on how long the offer will stand should not last any longer than 2 weeks.

Reflection Questions:

1. What would you change if you had a chance to do this event again?

_____

_____

_____

_____

_____

_____

_____

_____

_____

2. What's one goal you would like to set for the next event?

_____

_____

_____

_____

_____

_____

_____

_____

_____

_____

3.  What things might you want more
    help with?

_____

_____

_____

_____

_____

_____

_____

_____

_____

# 9

# WHAT'S NEXT

Now that you have created a blueprint for your next epic event. Take the next steps and download a free event planning checklist. Visit www.MelissaJakes.com to

Grab your checklist Now!

## ABOUT THE AUTHOR

Melissa A. Jakes is a Washington, D.C. based event planner for entrepreneurs, influencers, and a speaker who has spoken at several college/university and nonprofits organizations. Best known for being the "Olivia Pope of Live Events," was featured on Amazon's New releases and was place #2 for multiple weeks. She has been featured in the film "STEP", Event Planner Association Podcast, and The Baltimore Sun. Melissa Jakes was born and raised in Maryland. You can visit her website here: www.MelissaJakes.com